KINGSBARNS GOLF LINKS

The 8th & 15th greens.

KINGSBARNS
GOLF LINKS

Photography **Iain Macfarlane Lowe & Christopher J. Lowe**   *Author* **Malcolm Campbell**

The par three 15th tee to green

Published by

Kingsbarns Golf Links

Kingsbarns

St Andrews

Fife KY16 8QD

UK

Web site

kingsbarns.com

Copyright and Credits

©2014 Kingsbarns Golf Links

Photography & Concept Iain Lowe Photography

Author Malcolm Campbell, Golf Writer

Black & White illustrations David Joy, Golf Historian

Kingsbarns medals & snuffbox Peter Crabtree, Golf Historian

Architect's 2nd hole plan Kyle Philips, Golf Course Architect

Book Design Savitski Design

ISBN 978-0-9571586-0-3

CONTENTS

INTRODUCTION

Along the rugged coastline of the ancient Kingdom of Fife, golf has its historical and spiritual home where the essential elements of links golf in its truest form are found. From the sandy soil that supports the fine fescue turf, to the broad sea views and undulating coastal features that run down to the sea, Kingsbarns Golf Links embraces this Scottish links heritage with a history reaching back to 1793.

In the two-plus centuries since, the game has been interrupted twice at Kingsbarns but the enduring characteristics of the site ensured that golf would always return to this superbly endowed links.

When Kingsbarns Golf Links reopened in 2000 it was little wonder that a golf course based so solidly on its Scottish links roots was greeted with such wide international acclaim.

This book follows the journey of the recreation of traditional links golf at Kingsbarns and the vision that made it possible. We hope you enjoy the journey and, more importantly, the golf course that emerged from it.

Kingsbarns caddies and golfers on the 15th green

HISTORY

Kingsbarns is a community with a long and romantic history. It takes its name from the 11th century when King Malcolm of Scotland commanded that his subjects' taxes, collected in the form of grain, be stored in great wooden buildings or 'barns' on land at Cambo Estate where Kingsbarns Golf Links now stands. The barns were almost certainly part of a fortification built against the marauding Vikings of the time.

However, there was a community long established on this idyllic stretch of coastline even before Viking longboats landed on Scottish shores. An ancient grave was discovered during construction of the golf course confirming a direct link to Bronze Age man 2800 years ago.

There is golf antiquity aplenty here too. Before the end of the 20th century the Kingsbarns Golf Club was already looking back on more than two hundred years of the game as one of golf's oldest clubs. It records its history from September 4, 1793, when the Kingsbarns golfers were recognised by their next-door neighbours at Crail Golfing Society and granted permission to wear their distinctive blue jackets alongside the scarlet tunics of their compatriots on Crail's Balcomie Links.

The Kingsbarns Golfing Society, as it was named initially, already had its own emblem although the society was not officially founded until 1815. The date is confirmed on a silver jug, pictured right, presented by the members to Thomas Erskine, the 9th Earl of Kellie, in recognition of his generous donation of a dining hall and land for the nine-hole golf

PRESENTED BY THE MEMBERS OF THE
KINGSBARNS GOLFING SOCIETY
TO THE
RIGHT HON.ble THOMAS NINTH EARL of KELLIE
IN THE TESTIMONY OF RESPECT FOR HIS GENERAL CHARACTER AS
NOBLEMAN, GENTLEMAN, LANDLORD AND NEIGHBOUR
AND MORE ESPECIALLY IN ACKNOWLEDGEMENT
AND GRATITUDE FOR HIS LIBERAL KINDNESS IN HAVING
SINCE THE ESTABLISHMENT OF THE SOCIETY IN
GRANTED THE USE OF HIS LINKS FOR THE EXERCISE OF GOLF
AND ERECTED IN 1826
A DINING HALL FOR THEIR ACCOMODATION.
THE CUP WAS PURCHASED IN 1939 TO REPLACE THE ORIGINAL
WHICH WAS DESTROYED BY FIRE IN 1938

WON BY
William Clark, Hillhead 1823
Richard Todd, Balcomie 1824
William Clark, Hillhead, 1825
David A. Lindsay, of Lochton, 1826
James Wilson, Kinglassie 1827.28
David A. Lindsay, of Lochton, 1829.
David A. Lindsay, of Lochton, 1830.
James Wilson, Foodie, 1831.2.
Alexr Latta, Kingsbarns, 1833.
William Aitken, Thirdpart, 1835
John Clark, 1836.7.8.9.40
Wm Clark, 1842.

The Spring Meeting of Kingsbarns Golfing Society was held Saturday Last (the 3rd). That day being favourable, the muster of members on Cambo Links at 12 o'clock was pretty numerous and several well contested matches were decided. In the afternoon, the Club sat down to an excellent dinner in the house of Mr Brown, Vintner, Andrew Corstorphan Esq in the Chair.

After the cloth was removed, the health of the King and many loyal and sentimental toasts were drunk; interspersed with several good songs. At 6 o'clock, The Secretary, according to the rules laid down by the Society, proceeded to transact their business by reading over the minutes of the former meeting, collecting forfeited bets, entering new members and taking on new matches for the next meeting; which being concluded, at the suggestion of one of the members, it was unanimously resolved to provide the Society with a medal, to be competed for by the members annually, and a committee was appointed to carry this resolution into effect by the Lammas Quarter. After spending the evening with that sociality and harmony which uniformly characterises this Society, the company separated, highly satisfied with the day's entertainment"

Extract from *The Fife Herald*, May 8, 1823

course.

This magnificent silver trophy, and the medals played for by the members at the time, points to a wealthy and influential club very active in the formative years of organised golf in Scotland.

There was something of a setback in 1844, however, when a local farmer decided to end the long-standing land dispute he was having with the Society by ploughing up the golf course! Soon afterwards the Society suspended operations, gathering its records and medals together and sealing them in a box.

It was nearly 80 years before the box was reopened and Kingsbarns golfers returned to their links when, on 10th November 1922, the present day Kingsbarns Golf Club was formed. They played again over their own course until part of it was taken over by the military at the beginning of the Second

World War. There was a brief resumption of play at the end of hostilities, but in 1948 the course closed once more, and was to remain so until the end of the century. The Club moved into a joint arrangement with its neighbours at Crail to play over Balcomie Links, although its members also enjoy playing annual events over the newly established Kingsbarns Golf Links.

Today strong echoes of the past are still heard around Kingsbarns Golf Links. When visitors make the short journey from the 18th green over the ancient burn and across the bridge built by French prisoners during the Napoleonic Wars, they walk with the ghosts of golf past and with the hand of history a light touch on the shoulder.

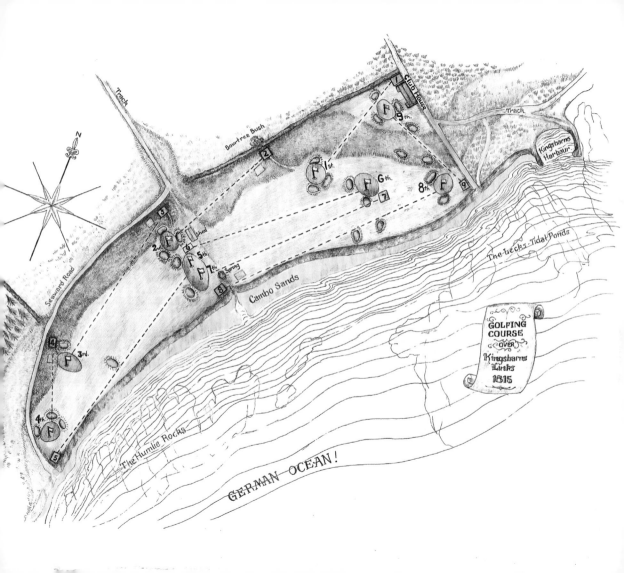

GOLFING
COURSE
OVER
Kingsbarns
Links
1815

A LINKS REBORN

The potential to create a world-class golf course was immediately obvious to Mark Parsinen and Art Dunkley when they joined forces with course architect, Kyle Phillips, to bring about the rebirth of links golf at Kingsbarns.

Phillips' clever routeing plan combined with Parsinen's inspirational input to the design detail ensured that the core imperative of creating a golf course true to the spirit of the traditional game was not only achieved but in many ways surpassed.

Kyle Phillips' plan for the 2nd green

Parts of the original layout from 1793 were incorporated into the design and an important and inspired decision was the acquisition of additional land to build the now world-famous 12th hole.

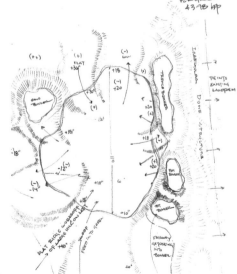

It was not the easiest site to work but the natural amphitheatre, created by the two-tiered aspect of a site that meanders along the seashore and also steps back from the ocean up and over rising ground, made possible a wide and captivating panorama.

The abundance of free-draining soil ensured that all the key elements of the authentic links experience could be built into the golf course and it is a testament to the design that so many visitors comment that the course "looks like it has been here for a hundred years."

The view of the 2nd tee to green prior to construction

KINGSBARNS TODAY

Since it opened for play again on 17th July 2000, Kingsbarns Links has rapidly risen up the wish lists of 'must-play courses' for many golfers worldwide. As the course celebrated the start of its second decade it reached a significant milestone, hosting more than 300,000 rounds of golf since it opened.

Kingsbarns has been recognised by the golf media from its first day of re-opening. For example, *Golf Digest* heralded Kingsbarns as the "Best New International Course" in 2000 and has continuously since 2001 rated Kingsbarns in its Top 100 Worldwide (54th in 2011), *Golf Magazine*'s "The 50 Greatest Courses Created in the Last 50 Years" 2009 list ranked Kingsbarns No 1 in Europe, and for 2012, once again *GolfWeek* ranked Kingsbarns as No 1 on the Great Britain and Ireland Modern list of courses built since 1960. In 2011, for the fourth time in its history Kingsbarns was voted "Golf Course of the Year" in the Golf Tourism Scotland awards, recognised as the Home of Golf's industry Oscars.

While it takes great pride in these awards, Kingsbarns Golf Links continues in its quest to further improve the unique Kingsbarns experience on and off the golf course. A genuinely warm welcome adds to the enjoyment of quality Scottish food, outstanding locker room facilities, and a highly regarded caddie team.

At Kingsbarns Golf Links visitors enjoy the welcome and facilities equal to an exclusive private members' club and benefit from the ultimate golf experience open for all to play.

The completed par three 2nd tee to green

THE FRONT NINE

For the visiting golfer, the excitement and anticipation of Kingsbarns Golf Links begins immediately with the drive through the entrance gates down the winding driveway to the imposing stone-built clubhouse standing proudly on a headland overlooking the sea.

From the first tee there is a growing hint of what to expect, with the eye drawn down a wide and rolling fairway that invites a confident opening drive to set the scene on a front nine that runs down to the sea, and which tests and teases shotmaking and the visual senses in equal measure along the way.

By the time the journey across fast-running fairways and over large and tempting greens returns almost imperceptibly to the headland, the warm welcome of the halfway house is there both to offer an opportunity for reflection and to whet the appetite for what is yet to come.

An aerial view of the par five 3rd and par four 4th holes.

HOLE

1

The gently sloping fairway of the 1st, with the backdrop of the Firth of Tay and the Angus hills beyond. The black and white post indicates a line to the left of the direct route. A warning hint of a bunker lies to the right.

The wonderful panorama that greets the player at the Par 3, 2nd hole offers a dangerous threat to the high level of concentration that this beautiful but always testing hole demands.

The 3rd hole marks the arrival at sea level and the first Par 5. To the right the waves crash on the rocky shoreline while to the left the sharply rising ground can be used to good advantage from the tee. But this initially and outwardly docile hole harbours the potential for high numbers if it is not granted a full measure of respect.

Its teeth lie in the dangers of too bold a second shot that must either find the sanctuary of the green if the drive is long enough, or, more likely, be positioned to find the safest approach to a double-tiered putting surface that slopes wildly from the left and cries three-putts from almost any angle.

The cavernous bunker (pictured below) that starts well short and right of the green, and stretches forward to eat into the green itself, must be avoided at all costs. Only perdition awaits within its sandy jaws.

HOLE

4

The short walk up the embankment to the 4th tee once again mischievously denies any view of the sea, but returns it spectacularly with the view from the upper level.

Here we find classic risk and reward with the option of a drive safely to the gap to the right side of the fairway, or to boldly try the tempting carry across a fearsome bunker much wider than it looks. The safe tee shot presents a more testing approach to an infinity green exposed to the vagaries of wind from whatever direction it blows.

The 5th presents another example of the requirement to carefully manage risk and reward at Kingsbarns. This short Par 4 opens with a tee shot toward the horizon, since the green is hidden from view. Fortunately the fairway is more generous to the left than it first appears.

The infinity green of the previous hole is followed here by an infinity fairway with a broad view of the North Sea beyond. A bold and long tee shot will leave a much simpler attacking shot to a difficult and wickedly sloping green, but stray too long and too far left and par will almost certainly be out of reach. Careful placement from the tee leaving a longer approach is usually the best advice.

HOLE

5

The crumpled contours that make the
5th green such a challenge.

HOLE

6

A short walk from the 5th green surrounded by high dunes to the perch of the 6th tee reveals one of the most dramatic views at Kingsbarns, while the tee shot is one of the most tempting.

HOLE

7

The long two-shot 7th is the toughest of the Par 4s on the front nine. The uphill approach is both long and demanding and any par scored here is a victory to be savoured.

HOLE

8

What devilish cunning has been built into this innocuous looking short Par 3 with its backdrop of sea and windswept woodland. Played downhill to a double-tiered green that feeds from right to left, the challenge is not of length but of control to find the correct level. With the pin to the left the contours can be harnessed to concede a birdie opportunity, but failure to hold the top level when the pin is to the right places a demand on the putter that only the soundest touch will survive.

HOLE

9

The front nine concludes with this long Par 5,
frequently played into a headwind.

Lee Westwood famously holed his second shot here at the 9th for an albatross on his march to victory in the 2003 Dunhill Links Championship.

THE BACK NINE

O n the back nine at Kingsbarns we can touch the vision that moulded farmland into linksland leaving behind a rumpled landscape redolent of much more ancient golfing ground.

Here there unfolds a glorious amalgam of the meeting of rugged coastline and the vision of the human mind that creates something timeless.

The 12th and 15th holes are perfect examples. Both became world-renowned on the instant that flagsticks were first inserted into the ground.

From the 10th to the formidable challenge of the 18th and the crossing of the historic bridge, the back nine at Kingsbarns presents a journey of trial and sometimes trepidation; a communing with nature that is as exhilarating as it is stirringly emotional.

The approach to the par five 12th green.

The welcome of the halfway house beside the 10th tee allows time for a little respite but no opportunity for complacency. There are no bunkers on the journey to the green but finding the best route over and around the swales and hollows that culminate in a putting surface of fiendish cunning, requires guile and a steady nerve.

The fairway bunkers at the 11th are spotted from the tee easily enough. Avoiding them is another matter entirely. The challenge is the approach to a huge green that has the capacity to shed the ball from its surface like water from a pitched roof.

The view from the 12th tee to the distant green
is one of the most memorable in golf.

It is a gentle walk to the 12th through woodland and over bridge and stream and where again the ocean is stolen from our gaze. When it is given back at the top of the incline at the tee the assault on the senses is often difficult to believe. The spectacular view of course and coastline is the one instantly recalled by many long after they leave Kingsbarns.

Here we find not only one of the most memorable of the world's great three-shot holes but one that cunningly conceals iron within the velvet glove.

Beware the temptations of the left; far better is the relative safety of the right. However, with a green more than 75 yards long there are many dimensions to the choice of shot, setting a premium on touch and dexterity.

HOLE

13

The third of the Kingsbarns Par 3s is another of less-than-daunting length. Again, the views of sea and coastline must at least be temporarily pushed to the side until the business of finding a way to this often-elusive green is found. The wind is a subtle and critical factor here.

Long is marginally better than short on a green that is deeper than it looks from the tee, but in left or right there lies very little hope of a par figure.

Careful placement of the tee shot, to avoid the dangers
to the right and the deep bunkers restricting the
landing area, offers at least a realistic chance of a birdie.

HOLE

15

The beauty of the famous 15th hole at Kingsbarns is only
ever overshadowed by the severity of the challenge.

Again the view of the sea is lost with the short walk down to
the 15th tee but when it returns it is not only spectacular but
intimidating in its prospect. The direct road to the sanctuary of
the green lies over rocks and an expanse of the North Sea with
a carry progressively longer to the right. A more conservative
approach from the left must flirt with trees and a deep bunker.
But the green is larger than it looks from the tee and boldness
combined with a steady hand will often bring just reward. This,
the most testing of the Kingsbarns one-shot holes, is already
a classic and another of the top contenders for the visitor's
memory bank.

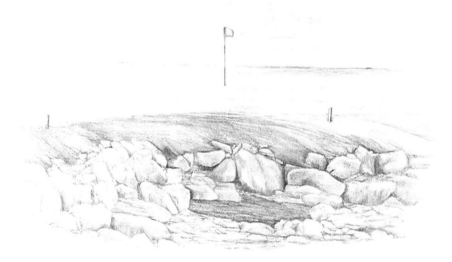

HOLE

16

The beautiful rolling fairway of the 16th is partially and tantalisingly blind from the tee.

The last of the Par 5s at Kingsbarns follows the curve of the bay along a rumpled but generous fairway pockmarked with deep and punishing bunkers. Danger lurks not only from the slightly blind tee shot that needs to favour the left, but also in the layup to a green that is rarely accessible in two against the prevailing wind. Subtle slopes and a pronounced swale characterise the putting surface, with a sting in the tail for a shot too bold in the form of a burn hidden from gaze that winds its way behind the green ready to gather and punish.

HOLE

17

Here the choices of risk and reward are straightforward. Carry the bunkers from the tee and rejoice in a much easier approach, or face a long and difficult shot from the left to a sloping, multi-tiered green.

The 18th is always one for the memory bank when visitors play out the final drama at Kingsbarns. A tee shot must be long enough to offer the chance of reaching the green in two. Then a final risk and reward decision becomes obvious–to try to carry the 18th century 'cundie' built by the French prisoners, or to lay up short and try to make par with a difficult pitch and putt. The eyes of those who have only recently undertaken the adventure look down from the clubhouse windows with much more than passing interest.

The walk across the ancient bridge can reveal much about success or failure on this, the final stage. But, whatever the result, the warmth and camaraderie of the clubhouse offers the perfect atmosphere for reflection.

HOLE

18

Perfect harmony: Kingsbarns Golf Links, where
the future blends seamlessly with the past.

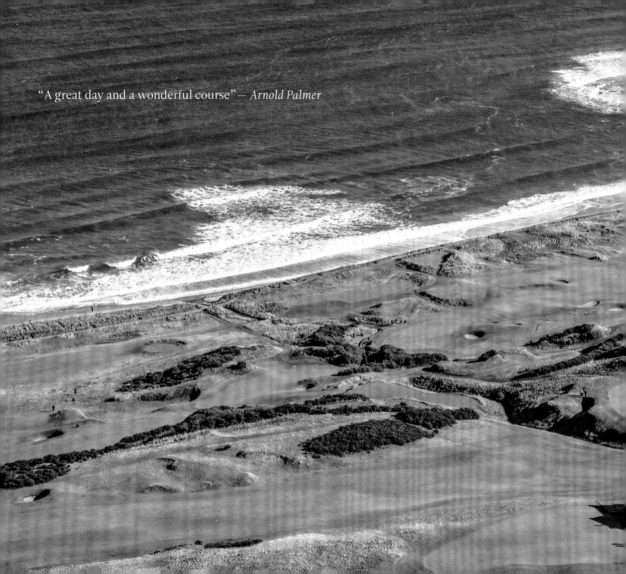
"A great day and a wonderful course" — *Arnold Palmer*

THE ALFRED DUNHILL LINKS CHAMPIONSHIP

Better known as 'The Dunhill' this annual end-of-season celebration of links golf is played over Kingsbarns Golf Links, the Old Course at St Andrews and Carnoustie. Since it was first played in its current format, offering one of the richest purses on the European PGA tour, it has attracted many of the world's greatest players including Lee Westwood and Colin Montgomerie and majors winners such as Rory McIlroy, Fred Couples, Darren Clarke, Ernie Els, Retief Goosen, Nick Price and Vijay Singh.

Many celebrities and famous names from the entertainment world including, to name just a few, Hugh Grant, Bill Murray, Andy Garcia and Michael Douglas have joined the professionals over the years in the pro-am element of the event that features individual professional and team tournaments.

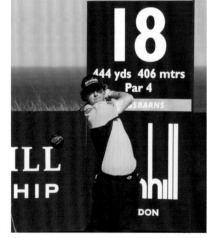

2011 US Open Champion Rory McIlroy MBE

18
444 yds 406 mtrs
Par 4

KINGSBARNS

dunhill

LONDON

*Four times Major winner Ernie Els, a regular
at The Alfred Dunhill Links Championship*

Robert Karlsson in trouble at the 18th watched by Colin Montgomerie during the 2011 Alfred Dunhill Links Championship.

The rising sun heralds another memorable day at Kingsbarns Golf Links

From Mid-November until the end of March Kingsbarns Golf Links dons its winter coat and enjoys a well earned rest and occasional snow fall.